Rain Season

Robbie Coburn lives in the small farming district of Woodstock in country Victoria. His poetry and critical work has appeared in a variety of publications including *Unusual Work, Going Down Swinging* and *Rochford Street Review*. His first chapbook, *Human Batteries*, was published by Picaro Press in 2012. *Rain Season* is his first full collection. Find him online at www.robbiecoburn.com

Robbie Coburn

Rain Season

PICARO PRESS

Acknowledgements

Some of these poems have previously been published, sometimes in slightly different form, in *Going Down Swinging*, *Unusual Work*, *Regime Magazine of New Writing*, *Voiceworks*, *POAM* and in the chapbook *Human Batteries* (Picaro Press, 2012). Grateful thanks to the editors. Some have also appeared, often abridged, in the public art exhibitions *Sites to Be Seen: Personal Art in Public Places* and *Eppicentric: Rereading the Signs*. Special thanks to Sandy Caldow.

The final stanza of 'The Paddock' was inspired by Robert Adamson's poem 'The River'. 'Becoming a Time Capsule' borrows a line from Harry Fainlight's poem 'Wolstonbury'.

Special thanks to Rob Riel for publishing this book and so much other worthwhile Australian poetry.

Thanks are due to the numerous people and poets who inspire me most, particularly Ashley Capes, Anthony Lawrence, Elizabeth Campbell, ∏. O., Sandy Caldow, Robert Adamson, David McComb, Maria Olsen, Peter Hitchener, Philip Larkin, Rae Desmond Jones, Geoff Lemon, Byron, Rob Riel, Mark Roberts, Jeremy Kewley, Harry Fainlight, Allen Ginsberg, Nathan Hondros and countless others, dead and alive. Sharon, John, Matt and David Coburn, who were always there. Suzanne, Margaret and Jack Coburn, my other mothers and father. Sophie Baker, Kaylen Court, David Rankine, Rachel Williams, Judita Turco, Ruby Rees-Wemyss, Jarrod Lappin, Brooke Grimes, Katelynn Jones, Bethany O'Conner, Lou Verga, Jack White, Matthew McAleer, Samantha Baker, Loretta Lackner, Anne Fraser, Nikki Thomas, Lily Meighan, Amanda May. And everyone else I've met and everyone I haven't yet.

Also due thanks to God for persisting with me.

Rain Season
ISBN 978 1 921691 65 2
Copyright © text Robbie Coburn 2013
Cover Image © Sandy Caldow 2013

First published by Picaro Press 2013

This edition published 2015 by
Picaro Press – an imprint of
GINNINDERRA PRESS
PO Box 3461 Port Adelaide 5015 Australia
www.ginninderrapress.com.au

Contents

I. Woodstock	9
Woodstock	11
Shed Music	12
Sophie	13
Boyhood	14
There Are No Strangers	15
A Lonely View	16
Germ	18
The Sleepwalker's Journal	19
The Pup	20
Race One	21
At the Greyhounds	22
Dog Fight	23
The Slip Track	24
The Brindle Dog	25
The Music of Running in Circles	26
The Heart Resetting	28
Dirt	32
Flame Tree	33
A Target in the Clearing	34
The Paddock	35
Life in Decay	36
II. Rain Season	39
Rain Season	41
III. Becoming a Time Capsule	49
Becoming a Time Capsule	51
Chemical Winter	52
Suicidal Years On	53
Sleeper Song	54

Demo	55
The Measured Spiral	56
Poem	57
Follow	59
St Mary's	60
The Murder	61
Three Lessons Remembered	62
A Ghost Story	64
Last Round	65
Drunk Dial	66
I Used to Know Myself	67
My Beer Belly	68
Sonnets for Sophie	69
Rain and the Dark	70
Comments for Anxiety	71
Slice	72
Fresh Burn	73
Two Lies in Sequence	74
The Tunnel	80

For ∏. O.,
Sandy Caldow
& Elizabeth Campbell,
with love and thanks

Then I will give you rain in its season,
the land shall yield its produce, and the trees
of the field shall yield their fruit.

Leviticus 26:4

I. Woodstock

Woodstock

back inside the property, a decay brought by seasons;
paddocks eaten into harvest are still,
brown soil dreams of green, aged stalks swinging
from the earth, beaming out of charred yellow wounds,
old structures: plump as berries on the land,
stand in place.
a weary farmer walks two greyhounds
down an alleyway, halting
to piss beneath a silo,
his folded eye stretching borderlines from the shade.
today comes a vision stuffed into silent growth;
farmlands in development have met the city,
Woodstock, masked, breathes from her sleep
pushing smoke down a busy asphalt road.

Shed Music

my generation don't read poetry –

poetry: inescapable vice, soft sky-call
& murmur
sung in whispered ticks building
to break through heaven back to earth.

from the window, the pulling tranquillity
of rain, a midday shower –
circles of mist pelt down on the tin silo,
shed music plays –
a process set in its seasons.

through the fall
dogs comb their runs for cover,
barking at clouds hanging from a full,
murky sky,
the following sun scaling dirt,
filling circled prints left by frantic hooves
of mares making rounds
in the paddocks

until soon, a lull presents
an opening within this state of solitude:
details amplify air, capture motion,

a poem births itself from the earth.

Sophie

you are lying
in a paddock

your smile

softens amongst the grasses

wind braids your hair

the earth is happy
beneath you.

Boyhood

tonight a round moon lies
in the centre of the dam
behind my grandparents house
worming into place between reeds,
spade trenches & rock embankments.

dark has an agenda out here
perched unapologetically on the tin roof
to remind the residents it belongs.

my window blankly watches
night enter its screen
as pale and black-holed spectres
pull faces at the wind,
immune to this veil of sky.

a familiar mist sets in over our farm.
the greyhounds restlessly expect morning.
my mother stirs alone in the next room.

I listen to the buzz of the old radio
outside in the shed where you work
and will stay until morning,
your footsteps breathing patterns
into the airwaves that sound,
build in volume.

There Are No Strangers

there are no strangers past the lookout post of the farm;
in blankets, the kids size up soft-storm path.

dogs bark away below the hill
drowned out by puttering drops in miniature springs –

both earth and sky still in the former absentee's wake –
trees shake hands. rocks run a marathon,

finishing up by the veranda, still
alive and ticking like an electric fence.

night encases the empty sky, indistinct amidst symphony.

home suspended on brass hinges,
I ignore all motion. alive.
my hands have disappeared in front of me –

there is beauty in that.

A Lonely View

all day I had scratched at the glass
and watched acres shrink in the
drying light.

timed gusts of stale air
lined with smoke
rose from red-dust roads,
the widening of dirt surfaces
as the city scaled sleeping
properties.

asphalt and stone
swallowed everything.

blackened clay pinned to
reduced dams, a perturbed
landscape thinning in the
unravelling winds.

as night fell, I combed
disintegrated ground for
any gathering of home,
the airless sky that once
held trees grew a skin

of smoke before
I watched the clouds light.

soon the grasses
became rubble, breath beaten
from my lungs, strangled
beneath the debris and embers
enveloping the house.

I gave myself to the fire –

as I died, weatherboard
piled in sheets of ash around
the darkening farmland –

the world was burning
and my father
had fallen asleep.

Germ

all things become dust;
cloud-veiled sky, moon already out
confusion blankets the property, miles
of thought folding into atmosphere.
we are young now:
a soft pull, cancer divides landscapes
our bodies decaying as we talk, grate
paddocks and smoke grasses.

we make our way back inside.
before the drugs take hold
time lapses around our youth. silence
then rain, heavy fall of rain and nothing
until night paints the light-flecked sky.

The Sleepwalker's Journal

smoke illuminates what it cannot define
as it rises from my fingers,
measured darkness filters through the sky's
focussing lens, the same night forever coming,
a sleepwalked path to the alleyway
preserving my footprints, chemicals slash
at unravelled membrane,
all is stilled on the farm but noise that prises
the air apart.

inside, my mother is crying,
cradling a child's bones in her arms
after he was found matted across
the concrete beneath the tenth floor
of a building in the city.
she calls to me and I remember.

sequences of flood enter the night:
in my lap, my arm is a cratered and faceless
moon, marked by explorers who's knives
are carried territory, pushed through
the waking universe as softened lines,
aimless attempts at change landing
only meters from the earth.

the weightless breath
embeds on my chest and pulls forward
the old dream of reversal, regret
stitched into stars igniting the galaxy
above the paddock.

laying across the world I realise
I have destroyed my life.

The Pup

the runt, thin as a wire in the straw,
lies on its side, apart from the others
who group around the bitch's naval.

cloak of night darkening the old horse stall:
milk fills new pups, while the stragglers berth
can only widen.

here I dream the runt boxes air:
nameless, voiceless, lifeless.

when it was expelled from the stall,
God let it melt by the fire,
inside. and straight after

I never again watched a dog
slip into the grey pull of morning.

Race One
        dogs

pour from   boxes

  like flakes
    in to   a

bowl of

        milk.

At the Greyhounds

after Mark Reid

somewhere around the bend
where man's eye sees blindness –
a disturbance in the sand.

the dogs bound forward leaving
all work and time
in the grains.

you wait there
commander
& trap your son.

you hold him there
as if your arms
were better years.

Dog Fight

inexperienced greyhounds trial
down the straight at Healesville.
two bitches:
one brindle, one black, kick-start
from the boxes in long strides,
stencilling marks into sand, tufts of fur
taut against opposition panting.

fixed on the mechanical rabbit,
they compete a first time.

in the catching pen the striped one latches
onto the coat of the other attempting to tear
at her arteries,
teethe the ticking throat.

they begin to spar.

this is instinctive, territorial.
and in the end the victor will be put to sleep.

The Slip Track

next thing, I'm boxed in
hands clasping leather ropes, watching dogs bound
forward in a pack behind the lure. the sand's uncollected
spray is cluttering in the track's barriers,
sheets of rain draw themselves onto a seamless sky:
spectators are few, only serious trainers etching times
into the grains, printed lines illuminating a future
before the bend.
these driving moments stitch themselves into history,
fleeting stillness amidst the rainfall, on the cusp
of becoming memory.
there I watched you box our two inexperienced dogs –
a father learning and teaching yourself, you empty
your eyes in circles, counting paw prints as seconds –
there are always too many or too few
until I catch them, signalling back to you from the other side,
and then, moments later, you have taken them from me,
stepping into your footprints all the way back
to the kennels to hose away wet sand from their coats.

everything you find here is sacred:
a drop of rain in the centre of the track.
squashed hot chip packets in a vacant stand.
a resting greyhound in the emptying yard.

similarly, you feel attachment to the stretch of sand
we've just walked.

The Brindle Dog

returning from Seymour, greyhounds listen to tires
grip and scatter rocks on the driveway, allowing
a round of barking to coincide with our arrival.
shade-veiled eyes venture from the kennels,
beyond the shed where we unpack meat for them:
red mince ice-stilled in plastic bags filling
the boot of the wagon.

inside, the brindle dog barks at a bitch in season
lying in the adjacent kennel, and then reverently
waits for food at the clink of bowls and thud
of gumboots –

he has learned ingredients are many
and the waiting is an unavoidable element
of the ritual, nose pressed through a gap
in the wire preceding paws rising and landing
like springs on kennel floors.

then next, the first clang of a steel bowl on concrete,
followed by the short-timed silence of feeding time.

stillness is beyond the brindle dog's practiced mouth
as he traces the surface of his water,
standing, head raised, from the gate opening
as a meal is placed beneath him.

his tongue is soon painted blood red
snout muzzled by frozen mince
pupils reflected on the bowl's silver edge:
all attention is zoned in on the task at hand.

The Music of Running in Circles

race night follows the storm-soaked working week –
a tractor's rust-flecked blades smooth the slush
as gates usher spectator's and share holders through,
domed nightlights blanketing the meeting
like a bright counterfeit moon.

even in blackness clouds overhang,
readily awash with dark rain due in unwelcome spirals
in late hours; bets screen from upstairs TVs, cigarette butts
line concrete walkways, familiar fog gushing from dry
and nervous mouths that jostle into place on the grass.

below, on the track, with its miles and moments of stretch:
the music of running in circles conducts the invasive buzz
of crowds; cheers, curses. even kids dragged along by parents
step briefly from their daydreams and fix on the lure,
observing the running greyhounds.

barriers seal the panting bitches in,
separating stand and sand as the last is called and silence
leaves its ecstasy on the cool air. soon
collar-bound hands border the catching pen, dogs
nosing the winning post before the tail end falls through –

'take care of your dog before all else' my father once
told me, 'there's time to react to the run later on.'
words mirrored and engrained, these nights bring
memory, the past showered in a flourish
of rainfall. undoubtedly

I know, one day I will instruct my own son,
so that he understands:
before retirement or appraisal
all dogs must be trapped
and guarded by their owner's hands.

The Heart Resetting

1

my days return to the property
                        so all I have lived terminates here
half the case for my father who has travelled –
the dull and ageing fences sway in the dry wind
paddocks full of footprints and horse shit
wheels drive the siren closer once he has collapsed
inside the shed
tunnels of smoke rising from the fireplace
his heart has filtered thin drifts of life from the air
the house has filled with absence, with loneliness
the divide bridged only by my mother's forced
reassurance
I stay awake that night talking to his ghost until drink
floods my veins, praying to a God I hate.
dim stars hang from the gutters of the shed outside
my bedroom window
no moon shapes or separates the scattered skylights.
I cry for my failure as a son and slash my arms
with an old box cutter to die before him.
when I finally sleep I dream of his lifeless white body
beside mine
I tell him I love him and that I'm sorry
night fades in and out, whisper to whisper.

2

the men in our family can expect the failure
of the body,
the need of multiple bypasses to sustain
breathing and consciousness,
the chest heaved from its opening, the
collapse of an organ, silencing all motion.
vats of human blood line the walls
of hospitals as reminders.
bullet tubes pricking the skin, body resetting
its hourglass as the illness takes hold.
the open heart is probed by the surgeon's
knives and wires: they know
as well as we do
this curse is inherited, a root embedded
in the family tree.

3

my father won't look at me as we drive home
from the bus stop
I watch sheep and paddocks disappear out the window
houses slide in the other direction behind the thin fence-lines
conversation is stunted and forced between us.
I am tired of school and life: I decide I am tired of him too
he asks if I will help with the greyhounds
when we reach the house
when I say no he hits me properly for the first time in his life
his fist claps my shoulder roughly and I start to cry
his strained voice pressing my throat into the rear view mirror
when we get inside I change my clothes and walk out to the runs
where we slip our best race dog and feed the others
he forgives me and sits down to watch the races on TV:
it was all my fault and he is a good father.
Woodstock darkens beneath the recycled sky
I lock myself in my room after dinner and fall asleep
hoping I won't wake up but I know I will
it starts to rain outside, thick wires batter the roof above me
I hear the clang of tin as it hits the shed and silo
cold spirals shelter our farm, redirect the storm.

4

it was weeks before Dad returned home from hospital
and even then he suffered death a second time
spluttering beneath his gutted body, his chest's bloody centre
sewn shut.

cries rang through paddocks, dissolving into an empty sky.
smoking outside on that
first night of his second life, I watched the grasses bending in
the light, fading from my view.

Dirt

reading the dirt is easier after rain
rays of sunlight drying up hoof-prints
water stirring the eroded paddock

I think of light breaking against your body
months ago as we sat here
your fingers raking the clay, it crumbling

beneath your skin.

Flame Tree

for my mother

dusk collects the day's events
in a landslide of moonlight.
I lay against the runs smoking my last cigarette
as flies circle my head –
the wind stirs the grasses slowly,
breath loosed from my mouth
like unheard prayer to begin a new life.

the longing deepens until it collapses
in a culmination of urgency,
my body suspended from the high wires
like an ornament –
smoke clings to the paddock for years
after time is shaken, flakes
of ash gathered in the dirt
beneath your feet.

after the fire pulverises my branch
of the family tree, the gap allows
the sun to enter

to let you live, brighter beneath the
embers, carrying

my angry spirit, pushed through
the cracks in your mind into your
averted eyes, waiting.

A Target in the Clearing

six rifle shells slice the air at the back of the property
sleeping farmland stirs

a kangaroo, bounding through the clearing, buckles,
its gaze caught in the revolving lights of pillars angled
on either side of the paddock

the thud of its dropped body echoes, throngs of night trapped
in the sounding hail of an emptied barrel.

the farmer's eye scales the disturbed ground
clumping the swaying grasses to prise the animal free

snared in the flat patch beneath its weighted frame,
a head hangs from the opened naval, lolling and pulsing,
stunted limbs arched over the rimmed pouch of a target.

the rotating beams frame the lifeless bodies
tufts of fur parted around the wounds –
a circled furrow where a bullet pierced the heart
of the child whistles into the eye of the shooter.

his throat gathers a skin of frost, the lowered rifle lifeless
in his quivering arm. his eyes collect the night like trauma.

crickets scurry in the distance, wind snared
by the projected fray.
friction rings from the dragging cadavers as
warm tendrils of dry blood rise.

The Paddock

our lips are locked, bent together,
open mouths summoning the air in timed rushes

the tension between winds prises the sky open,
her eyes narrow,
a section of rusted yards appear in the distance.

stars hang on the low branches, leaves shifting
the galaxy above, gently in the gust
a strung treetop parts the greying clouds.

dusk filters between our linked fingers,
we stand in a paddock widening into a circled
track and watch the day shift into twilight.

wire fences run through her mystified eyes,
strands of her hair tangled in the swaying grasses.

over the farm
shadows blanket silhouettes in the drying air.
she steps closer and pushes her lips to mine

I love you.
I love you too.

the silvered half-moon stores her smile
and stormed eyes as her fraying body breaks

away, we turn back to the tree then each other
and are lovers, in this momentary time

though the wind turns the paddocks back
on itself, and at its edge
is the whole world.

Life in Decay

I will pass before the land –
before the city lines Woodstock's paddocks
and granite-seeded trees withstand autumn.
before farmlands are sectioned off by structures,
tires gripping concrete backyards, thick wires,
tram-lines weaving through dog runs, smoke
radiating in opposition to air –

I won't wait around for it;
a moment where reversal is transparent
and realised.

nineteen years I've waited,
waited for a lull, a lasting calm preceding
storm. each day it looms nearer,
creeping towards the blind property
as she sleeps, reflecting shade from her
centre.

Woodstock
Woodstock is decaying.

Woodstock
Woodstock is decaying.

all is beyond me now –
two decades of decay
will soon join the asphalt road to
Whittlesea.
I won't see thirty years, twenty,
intervening before the changes;
passing beneath the grasses of
Donnybrook crushed
by new houses.
the world will be one city;
stone and glass.
skyscraper's stirring the land,
winds rising in circles of smoke.
counterfeit livestock, lengths of land
full of all things man-made.

Woodstock
Woodstock is decaying.

Woodstock
Woodstock is –

II. Rain Season

Rain Season

i.

shopfronts are walkthrough time capsules here,
peeling paint mounted on old skin
roads snaking through a collage of development and rubble

asphalt stretches north to the city, veered off
into drought-stricken, masked towns
where Woodstock is Whittlesea is Donnybrook
is Kilmore is King Lake.

modern country Victoria:
December burns over, communities dry beneath a red
season, lands surface tipping to reveal cracked and rotting
undersides. yellow bush-grasses are frayed
in aftermath of fire, ground offloading pollen and ashes.

uncertainty is still homing, centuries revolving
in a combine harvester, south,
where the world is marked by third degree burns.

most of what is preserved is dust, industry sundried,
moth-eaten by heat waves,

eyesores protrude through cracks in the concrete,
local faces walk the broken footpath passed nostalgic
exhibitions where groceries
are sold, guided by new structures,

fast food chain restaurants, housing estates
have stripped and replaced paddocks.

a changed country wears a skin of ash, embers teeming
in wires of smoke, unfurling to blanket the charred
branches of trees.
fire gutters across the sky, the bush cremated, flared swirls
of fire boiling houses. the dead sleep through the inferno,
the wind sweeps the bones away

as the remaining township waits and festers
below the highway, thinning transparent rainfall on tin roofs

admitting strangers freely into this adjusting museum.

ii.

'the tyranny of distance is a foundation of farm life' –
words of my father seed the grasses and ring
through the paddocks as I walk, years later, wind
pulverising my bones.
the fire spared Woodstock that Saturday. why? why not us?
the heat burnt our faces as we listened, watched the flames
blockade time.

beauty is only set in stillness, height: the surrounding
shire is still black.
that night my girlfriend had called me and said
she was huddled beneath
a wet towel in a paddock beside family as the fire sank
deeper into bushland.
she was spared, and emerged changed from the flames,
her family pressed
into its scorched shell of memory.

King Lake has begun to dream green from rubble,
unfurnished paddocks west of Whittlesea irrigate the land,
a rush of wind clears this sideshow before
it can be captured. swiftly

fresh out of rebirth, beneath three years of harvest
charred bodies now line my dreams, screaming
from their thinning black shells. the dead are voiceless
after the fire has passed, it sweeps through again
in cycles, as night screens the sun and our museum
capsules the dark in wax.

iii.

frantic horses run down the Hume highway
to escape the fire front on Donnybrook Road
only to be booked by a hidden speed camera.

iv.

Saturday has turned the colour of darkness –
we were testing the height of the sky from the pool's edge,
connecting the cloud dividers with our fingers when the
embers swept through.

when the smoke first skinned the hilltops I was swimming
in Seymour, the annual event crushed in a murmured wind
from telephones.
the sirens were fading in the direction of home,
miles of land forced into the hopelessness of chaos.
the smoke-line scaped the surface of the water, drying
the basin as embers rose from the tile floor.

the tragedy then opened like a door, ajar for months –

we heard four houses had already gone up in Wandong,
the fire pulverising the shire's forests. livestock slept
beneath rolling sheets of dust beside their
owners, the godless air raking ash over the road-line.
the concrete blistered my feet as the crowd ran. I sank onto
the dried and burning lawn, some kind of friction piercing
lengths of asphalt as cars drove away. tears of ash engulfed
the collapsing weekend, grasses alight in a series of
smouldering dreamscapes.

so much fear, sky a mosaic of grey and black circles,
bridge to home reduced to rubble –
Saturday has turned the colour of darkness.

v.

tomb-sweeping hands trace the crumbling
gardens of King Lake,
it seeps into my dreams, floods of ash still collect
on Woodstock's yellow paddocks, only the remains
branding the property.

Madilyn's houses still stand, surrounded
by miles of charred forest
wolves scale the burial ground for bodies,
picking at the decaying bones.
carrion fumes into the air, drifts of rubble spill
into the off-run of seasons.
even animals are homeless, shelter staked out
in the surrounding towns.

dust circles continue to rise,
I remember loving her, our lives storming
from the blaze untouched, urgency unveiling
its portrait of rust.
(we have taken it all back now, leaving only piles
of bunt, unmarked bones)

her teenage voice quivers and falls from the phone,
eclipsing my ear.

her skin detached from its skeleton, words erase
in a gust of dream, her ghost enters my mind like fire:
a storm of ash hails, the point of forgetting
becomes a cornerstone of memory.

vi.

rain comes too late like a disorderly, drunken God,
mistimed wires driving days of burning to a close.
sheets and miles of fall, dark shades of rain
align the twilight.

water flushes from gutters, cascading off burnt tin rooftops.
a family walk through a house, cries silenced beneath
the smouldering shell. there is no memory left, dried
fragments of a past life collected in a blackened
photo album.

the unhurried storm pushes against the rings of smoke,
rolling beyond the trail night leaves in the belly of the farm.

squabbling cries carve into the darkness, an emptiness
that lingers, the voices of dead grandfathers rack
against the walls.

hours later, flames continue to bead through the roof,
immediate piercing thoughts reignite the fire.

they huddle inside the wreckage, breath quietening
the consistent drive
of questioning –

raindrops like knives
pierce the ground outside beneath

the slowly drowning sky.

vii.

along Grants road, out of Whittlesea anxious farmlands
again breathe last days of summer:
raised clusters of mud cake to an eroded fencepost,
frayed hay band crudely knots around dysfunctional
electric wire amplifying smoke signals ascending
from the calming fire front on Donnybrook Road.
clammy and blistered hands chop wood by the car bay,
hopeful preparations for a coming season.
horse floats shouldering dog trailers,
a farmer walks two buckets of water down an alleyway
to an old racehorse: he passes dry-hollowed, pale tanks,
yabbies make rainfall impressions on the dam
water's surface, a bay mare's hooves play billiards
with dirt fragments.

thirty acres down the road, on the next property
another farmer welcomes the scent
of a new rain in its season
walking through a paddock
asking questions the clean wind answers.

III. Becoming a Time Capsule

Becoming a Time Capsule

on an ordinary night it will happen:
the thud of a culmination
from the moon-silvered grasses
followed only by hours and years of
silence.
rapture stretches the length of sound
offering a sacrament to the sky's alter,
a pillar of mist eroding the landscape –

it will arise with becoming a time
capsule, never aged beyond impulsion
as year are cemented.

the deepest places lie open now;

a long dark: staggering off across
a space where the hills level, this is

an ache that will claw at the mind
and strike down the source of any
sanctuary

the heightened mound, a turret
entrenched further in the crossroad
of waking

as all longing pierces
consciousness,
leaping from this world to the next.

Chemical Winter

daylight bends like a flame
in a shadow-rinsed morning.
early showers sift away
the mind's reflection of storm clouds
as a chemical eclipses
the ache behind my eyes.

when night enters
I lay imprisoned by drifts of memory,
unsealed earth denying closure
from the wind's easy consultations
by the window. and still

dawn gathers thought before frost:
boundless floods of winter cover
acres of grass
beneath the dark's circuit of dead
echoes.

let the drugs probe at the radiating
cells to bring change.
soon, these cries that fall silent
upon warmer months.

Suicidal Years On

we woke to the ocean lashing
against the bay.
at its mouth a throwback stream
ripped into a tide
progressing to align a river.
we decided to trace the sea's throat.

a torrent of dark water
rushed over the riverbank.
we parted ways as the pool
deepened and rain built tensions
through the air, battering rungs of
greying cloud.

I heard about a boy
who was found face down in this river.
the stream had washed the blood and dirt
from his clothes.

the tide rips the foaming water
an opening where the calm air
enters.

it's inside me
in the sheets of wind
and lashing rains

it wants me to dress myself
in rocks and sleep beneath
the riverbed.

Sleeper Song

for Sophie

it's a shade that provides no shelter;
the warm light breaking against your body
platforms stirring under pasts of dust
progressing to align the skylight

all over, you sense whispered reassurance
singing softly from your skin
as openness presents its clock of frost
pulling you from this circle

here there is a longing in my blood:

the heart's resurgence that nets lovers
where your mind stills
framed ticks and traps ache infinitely
in your seamless plan of being

find your way back home
where night mirrors your moonless eyes,
empty your mind of its tyranny
here in the bed you dream from.

Demo

this is a song you love.
your coffee has dressed itself in skin.
it is a Saturday morning.
thin raindrops bead on the kitchen window.

bemused, I observe a dome sheltering
the basin of the mug:
the china has begun to set itself into
the table (you never use coasters)

burning an oak-brown ring on the cream surface,
an etching that resists materials and soaps or hides
beneath its stencil.
these details cross my mind as if only
to convince me they are the reason –
the reason I am unable to lift it, make it new.

The Measured Spiral

first strangeness linked to the
memory, then pain:

that play-thing, a hand dancing
beneath a belt buckle,
he slowly pulls at the seams of my body
until I unravel –
the remaining thread, tangled around his
blade, stills like water, leaving him
only monumental lengths of my skin;
sheets, nights and years of it.

years ago now, after I had survived, I asked
a shrink in the flat district for guidance –
I was instructed to tell her everything,
every raw detail until the flesh sifted from
my mind onto her notepad and changed.

I had to learn to love my forced hand and mouth,
rub and kiss my wounds as I measured the spiral.

so for the first time I didn't melt
with the feeling of when he first entered
nor the smell of beer, smoke, his taste and touch
or the length of his cock I felt at 12 years old

and as instructed, I now adore his Russian pocket
knife that branded my throat,

determining all that has followed.

Poem

there's a book about me I'm trying to write –
stormed eyes break first light
grey and yellow sent through the skies
gathered beneath a crimson sun,
marks etched into dawn.
early hours come, fresh –
nothing moves.
sound slices air from an opening.
here blood runs.

I open the vein, twice
the deeply pressed blade embedded
in flesh like an extension of my limb –
the frantic flow becomes a pool
in which I float
disturbing the drying red sea.

'Robbie, what have you done
to yourself?'

the discovery is short-lived and collected, a rise
of lines and ducts fallen from the empty
doorway.
this stalls death and suspends the image
that smoulders my body.
my burnt bones comb those of my
mother's father in swirling winds
inside the urn.

my family eye the forced tomb:
a cluster of ash gathers in the charred basin,
the clang of steel
projected in the bound container.

smoke is loosed from the oil lamp
radiating from the cooling hearth. thin
shadows fizz and break with the surge of
light worming through the furnace.
laughter rises between the flames,
the perished body a head-lining shell
scattered on floors, grasses and papers.
when I'm dead this will all make sense.

Follow

death was fashionable when we were kids –
on rainy days in king lake
shielded by the birch trees
we would walk the path to the door
of your backyard

where five years earlier your uncle,
stitched into his work shed, tied
a line of rope to the rafters
to suspend his body
and instruct you to follow.

St Mary's

i. confession

>Sunday service.
>blood thickens
>in the chalice.

ii. service

>the priest veils the front row
>with incense.

>behind the alter a face
>materialises,
>a blood sport.

The Murder

feathers rest beside you, confusingly still.
as always, it has escaped your mind:

out in the garden where the crows perch like towers.
love, each day I've watched it grow and become dust
as they feed with beaks and razor-sharp talons,
picking it away into nothingness.

lying in a bed of fractured, yellowed reeds,
dry soil and scattered, dying leaves are
black towers; you once looked out through
the kitchen window, smiling, love, smiling.
black crow perched on your heart, it feeds.
the dead shriek. the dead shriek, it flies,
marching like a guard to the watchtower.

death, black crow, death, you cry.
I swept your feathers beneath the carpet, black crow.
love, your garden has become overgrown left
unattended,

love, why do you still see roses?

Three Lessons Remembered

1. My First Time

I was fifteen the first time I tried
to die
drank my body weight in wine
from my parent's cabinet
& opened my wrists
with a razorblade
in the bath

thought of dad finding me
lying limp in the water
blood painting
the porcelain
around my body:
mulled it over in my head
until
it made some kind of sense

as I started to drift off
I thought of what comes
after we go
where our souls end up

I woke up in bed
on a Thursday

I've learnt you are only
allowed to die
when it's your time to.

2. To Be Gay In Kilmore

as a boy
thought boys were my thing
after a few quick shots
& smoked buds
we were up in the clouds quick;
so my friend Jarrod would do,
better than a random later on
at some party in Kilmore
I thought to give it a try
out to prove myself right
followed him from the room that night
my first brush with the other team –
I discovered girls were my thing:
his bearded mouth
just like kissing
a sewing machine.

3. Girls

the first girl I ever
lost sleep over
accidentally
rolled onto me
in the night.

A Ghost Story

they have other lives: illuminated
unseen resignations from being
bridges holed through to the other
side of waking

into the distance of continuous deaths
rusting in their ghostly chorus:
the slow, open gong of separation
and departure still sounds habitually.

this night, the moonlit road persists
into the twilight,
she pulls in and the car's ignition
of ticks switches to nothing

not gathered as she parks and abandons
the shell, a vibration dissolves
into the static skyline.

cars pass occasionally, engine's guttering
into the atmosphere, smoke only
mirroring the darkness.

the driveway's ceiling of footprints
filters the silence until it is almost
melodic –
she is never alone, sick with
the meticulous haunting of memory.
dreaming

till she foots her way to the house
to drudge up reality.

Last Round

reddened skin
clinks

against slate –

a makeshift pub
closes

with my eyes.

Drunk Dial

04*86
    5   7##*6
        4
56
    ##* 1
000

I Used to Know Myself

back in the days when fun meant fun
& love meant love
isolation wasn't a necessity
& it was possible to be off it long enough
for a hangover –
finishing sleep I walk the stretch of road
to the town centre to find the bottle shop closed.

back in sleep alone, it is late, room
widening to become worlds.

My Beer Belly

stares back from the mirror
bursting with all its acute toxins,
dreaming of another self –

thin as piano wire.

Sonnets for Sophie

I

on the last day of a Melbourne summer, sheets of rain fall
onto Burke Street, storm clouds lifting before returning
stitched to a full sky as thunder rolls like clockwork behind my eyes.
Sophie, you have extinguished the fires that became my mind
amidst flames I have dreamed you into being:
sun and colour wash through you in this summoning of water
your drenched body rising angelic from my skull.
cold wires paint asphalt, washed clean of ash and dying embers.
soon, very soon, love will shift with seasons as I wake –
time will take you from me, fire returning to claim my remains.
here is a moment I will keep. I hold your hand, fingers melding
our bodies as I kiss you a final time to the crackle of flames
looming below us. above, the continued drive –
your lips hands teeth, the rain.

II

were you scared of love that night?
these thorns rooted in the riverbed, dangerously hidden
propelling your fear into a frenzy. there my vices drowned
the ghost behind your eyes, the surface of your mind branded
only with soft rain and memory.
heat faded slowly from your body as pressure rose towards
the floodplain: we swam blindly, deeper into the oncoming storm.
waiting ahead, your voice almost fell silent under
the wind's growing echoes
and I was in love with you when you told me I couldn't be.
a kiss deepened into a disturbance in the water. you grew tired.
darker hours brought their wash of rain to bring floods,
a submergence, collapsing
your shade beneath the wires and streams.

Rain and the Dark

sleep, and forced thoughts of sleep come slowly,
air stilled, bottled by the weatherboard house
driving sheets of rain batter the tin roof, hours and miles
of night encasing the restless property.
awake, I scale visions like dreams, hope sinking
beneath the flood of rainfall in the blackness of my room,
Woodstock cowers under the weight of changing seasons,
the dogs bark against cacophony, silent prayers
for sleep drawn into a godless sky.
long hours press deeper, becoming a disturbance
in the land, invisible spirals teeming into hail.
a storm enters:
rain falls louder in the dark, sounding its soulless music
until dawn awakens.
morning will not come, only silence will enter.
again night allows no rest but fears that become my mind.
the ache grows, consuming the remaining drive of
contemplative
thought, recalling ambition and waste.
how hopelessly I move through the void of alone as I prepare
to cross into solitude.
the dark's soundtrack of rain pins atmosphere, consciousness
unravelling with the calculated stopping of breath.
the relief of sleep exists beyond being, only real
as it becomes eternal.
when death unlids itself, everything is better.

Comments for Anxiety

I certainly remember her name. and her face.
and her skin clamping onto mine that night
in June. but it's not even that we never slept
together. or that we parted quickly. or that
we never write that fixates my attention.
what I recall most of all is our separate
anxiety disorders that combined to drive her mad.

Slice

blood runs across the surface of my left wrist
& dances down to the carpet
doing the waltz without a partner.

Fresh Burn

upon returning from the city
the weatherboard house sheds its skin of rain.
a change of temperatures divides the farmland
and the fireplace churns smoke out like wind.

the septic tank buzzes, expected sounds amplified,
a pile of compost rearranges itself, lined by spiralling
overgrowth, most of the flowers have died or approach drying.
through the misted glass water evaporates in waves
of heat, steaming in front of acres of backyard.

the grass-ends sway on the paddocks separated by decayed
and unlevelled fence posts strung with tangled wires and electric
traps. I pick blindly at my left arm. immune to the forced scabs
a sudden prick of pain pulses from a carved furrow –
blood oozes in a circled hole where I'd crushed a cigarette.

I slide the window open and light up another.
pillars of smoke gutter into the shifting sky, adjoining
the city's sheet of mist. shadows gather on my lungs
as the bud crackles with the surge of orange flame.
clumps of ash shoot into the grass below the window sill,

I hover the stumped cigarette over my wine-red arm, predicting
the blistered tattoo, eying the wind that dances the branches
of a gum tree at the back of the property. after the burn, warming
air stings the skin in the centre of the weeping circle.

Two Lies in Sequence

depression.

I

everything is happening for a reason.

II

If our eyes
should scour lands, your irises
will always leave prints. Imprints.
Lies. Eyes. Lies. Memory.

Think back to
tomorrow, a year ago; leathery
hands, furry teeth, dilated pupils with
the ankles and toes sore.
I don't miss you (a lie).

III

The machine is lagging.
We, as cogs have called in sick yet again.
Dying; yeah, it ain't good but why worry
about it? The boss pulls out his hair,
we fly away to a holiday destination out
of our price range.

IV

Listen, pitch;
play the pipe of life
until the notes become flat
and you get fat
and you collapse.
Then that is that.

V

They're fucking in the back
of a pickup truck. (no no no)
She's fucking him not him. (what? no)
That morning, her husband had
accused her of poisoning his
breakfast. As if he would know,
like he would ever realise, eh?

If her heart strings still
sounded somewhat like
an out of tune harpsichord,
his madness would happily sign the papers.

VI

Oh to be mortal eliminates any chance of paradise.
(ha ha ha ha ha ha)

VII

Best avoid thorns, the creepers,
thrushes; they ensnare your
laces, binding them to the
undergrowth.
It's like the Earth, really. You
don't know where it'll bend
and give out. Roots intertwine,
you're stuck and your new
shoes are dirty. Shit.

VIII

Potholes. They are everywhere and each time I take a step
one of my feet falls quickly into the earth. I run, trying my
hardest to dodge the holes. My right foot slips. Shit. Step out.
Keep going. Left foot down fast as a rabbit. Step out. Step.
Fall. Step. Fall.
I look over the horizon towards the busy city There are
potholes everywhere the size of my feet but I keep going…
Going… Going… Going…shit.

IX

The house is empty. Better, he thinks,
having not thought of her
in days (another lie,
obviously).

X

Doctor: Good afternoon, sir, how are you?
Describe to me exactly what it is you've been feeling. They've
sent you here so that I can confirm you're crazy.
You are, sir, that's why you're here. Did you
not see the name on the front of the building?

'Go to hell, you sly bastard.
All of you go to
hell.'

XI

I breathe out of turn,
you shout, and I attempt
to cut my wrist with a
butter knife.

XII

Read The Bible before?
How sad is the bit when that magic man
is killed by being nailed to a cross for the
good of mankind?
A bit unrealistic and drawn out, if you
ask me, so I wouldn't recommend it.
Not enough action. Plus the author has asserted
far too many of his/her personal opinions on
the human condition. Steer clear.

XIII

Up a cliff face, reef below; clean, clear water.
Waves practically envelope the shore in the distance.
Take off your shoes, yes, your socks too. Why are
your eyes wet? Close them until they don't hurt
then let's play the risk game?

XIV

They are sleeping side by side,
clothes scattered about the floor. He'd
licked under the wings of her cunt after
dinner, the taste sweet as when they were
teenagers.

Sex is out of date. Expired.

XV

I don't have a woman. I don't drive a car.
Go on; tell me I'm a fucking waste of space.

XVI

fuck.fuck.fuck.fuck.fuck.fuck.fuck.fuck.fuck.fuck.
fuck.fuck.fuck.fuck.fuck.fuck.fuck.fuck.fuck.fuck.
fuck.fuck.fuck.fuck.fuck.fuck.fuck.fuck.fuck.fuck.
fuck.fuck.fuck.fuck.fuck.fuck.fuck.fuck.fuck.fuck.
FUCKFUCKFUCKFUCKFUCKFUCKFUCK***
****
****
****

XVII

BEST BEFORE
08/01/07   13:36

XVIII

Doctor: hghjghjbnmpol ptrog06mnkjkjm nmdskk1983 gfsaejnd hkjhkjyouhghjghffhbjhbfjuhbefare hguhfeppoqnqheyondsgyneidel,sbsag92nufnf bhjjbefjebfjedfdfdsjfffjusthjhjsjsjd,scrazyfnbv 9hbghgh3u833u4see?ggeufh. fuckfuckfuckfuck. youjhjhjnhjakkkkkmkdon'tknjknkjnkkkeven jhuhuih8jg16 b&jwk(nsm@ jkjkdodml, 0ph?hd bhhjbjjnjnjnjnknkunderstandhbhjbjdjndennnkk cscscsthis.kokiokokkppsp!nhkijkmjkmjkmjo989 u545dnkjnkkkmlmlkmllskj76jimsakam9nmahbq.

XX

everything is happening for a reason.

The Tunnel

shadow of the circled arc –
it bleeds from its centre
throwing light back, measuring
the tunnel as it deepens.

I want to be here, winding past
currents of depression
and venom,

black subway walls that
lead nowhere,
even if I could trace

depth beyond this before
oblivion starts to miss me.
inevitably

the familiar drone of void
will finish me, conclude
with suicide.
but when.

www.ingramcontent.com/pod-product-compliance
Lightning Source LLC
Chambersburg PA
CBHW071028080526
44587CB00015B/2541